CHANGING LANDSCAPES

ALEXANDER PECKHAM

GLOUCESTER PRESS
London · New York · Toronto · Sydney

CONTENTS

Chapter One
The making of a landscape 4
The Earth is in a constant state of change.
Landscapes are shaped over millions of years
by processes like erosion. Rapid changes,
such as earthquakes, also occasionally
occur, altering the lie of the land.

Chapter Two
The human impact 10
The natural development of landscapes
usually takes place very slowly. Problems
begin when the rate of change accelerates
because of human activities.

Chapter Three
Learning from the past 24
Human societies have existed for thousands
of years. Certain archaeologists argue that
the demise of some of these societies was
due to environmental destruction. Many
observers believe we may suffer a similar
fate unless steps are taken to repair the
damage we have caused.

Chapter Four
Changing our priorities 28
There are solutions to most of the
environmental problems we face, although
they may be difficult and costly to
implement. Changing our farming practices
and controlling population growth are two
ways we can begin to tackle the crisis.

Glossary 35

Index 36

▷ The rainforests that cover the tropical
islands of Micronesia in the Pacific Ocean took
millions of years to evolve. However, they can
rapidly be stripped away by loggers.

INTRODUCTION

A landscape is what we see when we look around us, whether we are in mountains, on rolling plains or in the heart of a city. No two landscapes will ever look exactly the same because each is shaped by many factors. These factors include rock type and formation, climate, plants, animals and human action; each place will have a different combination of these. Landscapes not only vary depending on where they are, they also change over time. New trees grow, rivers can change course or dry up altogether and new species may move into an area, pushing out the old ones. In some places volcanoes can change the lie of the land. Weather and the other forces which combine to structure landscapes are constantly changing. They are affected by the land itself, for example, when mountain ranges prevent clouds from passing over.

Humans have increasingly become the major agents of environmental change. Few places have escaped our influence. We usually describe most rural landscapes, such as the green, rolling hills of England, as "natural", but often people have played an important role in their formation. We have cut forests to make room for farmland or to graze animals and we have built homes, workplaces and roads. As long as changes do not damage an area and as long as they happen slowly enough to allow wild animals and plants to adapt, humans are merely influencing a system that is forever changing anyway. However, when changes occur too rapidly, species do not have time to adapt. Animal populations dwindle, plants die, soil is eroded and the landscape soon shows signs that all is not well. Today, technological progress, the growing population and overexploitation of resources and farmland are damaging the global environment. This affects all living things on the planet.

Chapter One

THE MAKING OF A LANDSCAPE

Every landscape is unique. Its character depends on a delicate balance established over thousands of years between the land and the plants and animals that live on it. This balance is not the product of chance; it is structured by the physical conditions that exist in a given place at a given time. The making of a landscape involves both daily occurrences, like rain and sun, and long-term change, like the creation and destruction of mountains. For example, plants have considerable influence on landscapes and their growth is dependent on the amount of rain that falls and the climate and soil. All of these determine where plants exist. In this way they influence the creation of a landscape.

△ This canyon in Utah was formed over millions of years.

How soils are created

Soil is essential in determining what kinds of plants grow in an area. It is a key element in structuring the landscape. Soil is made up of tiny bits of rock which have been broken down by wind, rain and snow over long periods of time. Each kind of rock makes a unique soil type. In addition, the same rock can produce different soils depending on the climate. Topography, the lie of the land, is another factor which affects soil type. On steep slopes, soil washes away quite quickly, exposing fresh rock to wind and the weather. In flatter

Without them, many mountain areas would lose their soil altogether and become barren, rocky deserts.

The lie of the land determines in turn some of the factors, like rainfall and sunlight, which shape the land itself. For example, hillsides may be in the shade for much of the day and not receive enough sunlight for many plants to survive. Also, high mountain ranges often prevent rainclouds from passing over them, affecting rainfall in the region. Much of Tibet is a desert because the 8,000-metre-high Himalayan Mountains block clouds coming from the south, thus preventing rain from reaching Tibet. In other areas vegetation can cause rainfall. Water evaporates from the lush tropical forests to create new rainclouds. Without rainforests there would be far less rainfall in many equatorial regions.

Long-term changes
We tend to think of a landscape as something static; permanent and unchanging since the dawn of the Earth. This is far from the truth. From the inhospitable and scorching wasteland that was the Earth's surface some 4,600 million years ago when it was first formed, the planet has changed a great deal. As the molten Earth cooled and the balance of gases which make up the atmosphere altered, life forms began to evolve, becoming ever more complex and diverse. During this process, landscapes changed beyond recognition.

Climates have always been altered by the slight shifts that occur over thousands of years in the Earth's orbit around the Sun. As climates changed during the Earth's lifetime, ocean levels rose to flood huge areas of land before receding, deserts were formed and then destroyed, forests grew up and died back again. Throughout this process, the evolution of life forms played

areas, the soil tends to remain where it is, and over the years, will be broken down further by the weather.

Although soil type determines where plants grow, plants also greatly influence the nature of the soil. For example, plants (including trees and crops) reduce soil erosion by binding the soil together with their roots. Dead vegetation that has dropped off the plants also helps to shield the soil from direct rainfall. Plants enable water to soak into the ground through the passageways their roots make; otherwise rain would just run along the surface and wash soil away. In hilly areas, plants are essential in holding soil on steep slopes.

Scientists believe that some 200 million years ago, one great land mass existed, called Pangaea. Since that time continental drift has carried continents to their present positions.

its part in altering the character of landscapes. New species of plants and animals emerged as old ones died out, and as a result, landscapes changed.

Of all the long-term influences on landscape, continental drift is probably the most important. Continental drift is the term which describes how the Earth's crust is continually changing as it moves across a layer of partially molten rock some 50 kilometres below the Earth's surface. Over millions of years continents break up. New oceans appear and disappear as the continents move around the surface of the Earth. When they collide, the Earth's crust buckles, forming new mountain chains. As the continents slowly move from cool to warm regions (or vice versa), climates change, and gradually new soils, plants and animals replace existing ones. These processes mean that all landscapes are temporary, evolving from the old and inevitably giving way to the new.

Rate of change

Natural changes to the landscape usually take place slowly, over thousands or millions of years. Only occasionally do more drastic changes occur; for example, when landscapes are mutilated by lava or ash from huge volcanic eruptions, or when pests like locusts rapidly multiply and destroy large areas of vegetation. Even when these dramatic changes occur, landscapes have an impressive ability to heal themselves. Fortunately, the fact that change is generally slow gives living things time to adapt to the new conditions.

On the time scale of the Earth's development, 10,000 years is a very short time. It is only 10,000 years since the huge ice sheets that covered much of Europe and North America began to recede. On and off for 600,000 years, vast areas now covered by grassy meadows, forests, villages and cities were barren lands of ice. To the south of these ice sheets lay treeless plains

△ This devastation caused by a volcanic eruption in Hawaii will soon heal.

△ Landscapes looked very different 100 million years ago when dinosaurs roamed the Earth.

dissected by streams fed by melting ice. Even further south lay vast forests of birch, spruce and pine. The deciduous (broad-leaf) forests that now grow in much of Europe and North America had retreated into areas like North Africa, the Middle East and Florida in the United States.

Only 10,000 years ago, therefore, many landscapes were radically different from those of today. The Ice Age left its imprint on the landscape in the form of valleys and hills carved by the great weight of advancing glaciers. As climates warmed, the ice melted except in the far north and south, and eventually the landscapes that surround us today emerged. Stone Age hunters migrated, following the animals they hunted. Plants also adapted to the climate change. Although some species could not survive, most struggled on and some actually benefited from the changes.

Since the end of the Ice Age, the world climate has remained relatively stable. But occasionally there have been major fluctuations such as the Little Ice Age in the 18th century which wiped out the Norse settlements in Greenland and led to the famous winter fairs on the frozen River Thames in London. However, despite the overall climatic stability, landscapes have continued to change dramatically. The landscapes we see today are significantly different from those created by the retreat of the glaciers after the last Ice Age. Forests have been cleared, rivers diverted and cities and roads have been built. Almost inevitably, human beings have been at the root of these changes.

Changing landscapes can be a signal that the environment is being damaged. In the worst cases, they can represent changing climates, eroding soils, altered vegetation patterns and so on. They can warn us that the complex interaction of the Earth's systems, which are necessary to support life, are being destroyed.

Controls on the landscape

Landscapes are forever changing. Volcanoes or severe storms can rapidly alter the land, but most of the forces which create and wear down landscapes occur over thousands or millions of years. The Earth's crust slowly folds and cracks as mountains are pushed up when plates collide. Climates change, taking the planet in and out of ice ages, and plants and animals adapt to the new conditions. Rivers carve canyons and the power of the ocean waves wears away coastlines. The daily action of the weather breaks down rocks to make soil, and determines where different plants can grow.

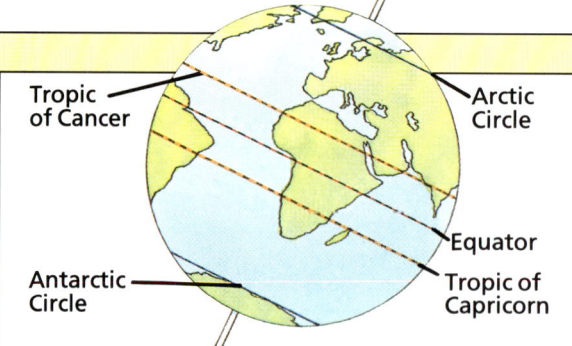

Latitude

Lines of latitude are imaginary lines which run around the Earth, parallel to the Equator. As the Earth spins and moves around the Sun, different latitudes receive varying amounts of sunlight, and the lengths of days and nights vary. This affects the climate in an area.

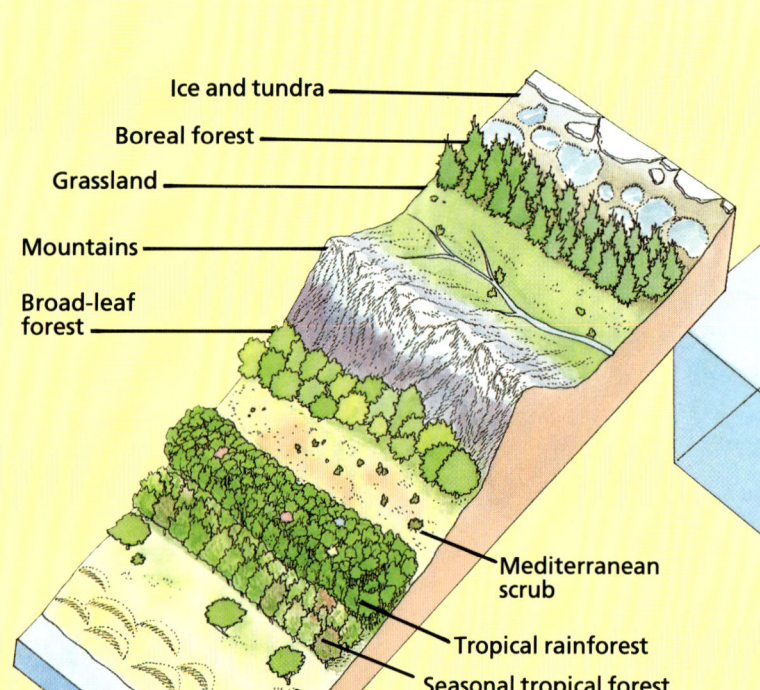

Ice and tundra
Boreal forest
Grassland
Mountains
Broad-leaf forest
Mediterranean scrub
Tropical rainforest
Seasonal tropical forest
Savanna
Desert
Sea

Vegetation

Habitats

The Earth has many kinds of different environments, called habitats. They range from the extremes of the frozen polar lands to the humid rainforests. Each has a variety of plants and animals which have adapted to its conditions.

Rivers

Running water erodes the land; many valleys are formed by the action of rivers.

Geology

There are many types of rock, each of which is formed by different processes. Rocks are the basis of the planet.

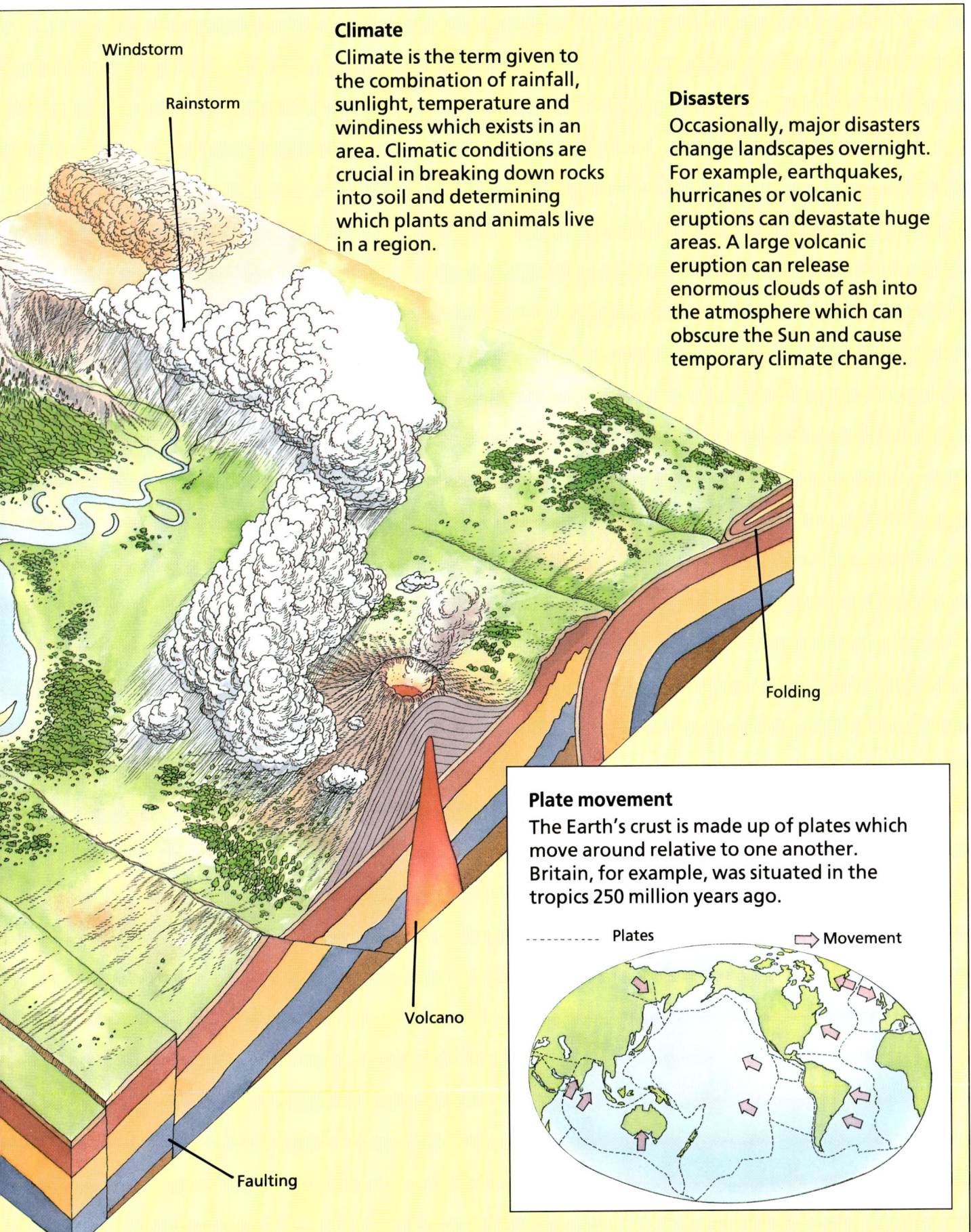

Climate
Climate is the term given to the combination of rainfall, sunlight, temperature and windiness which exists in an area. Climatic conditions are crucial in breaking down rocks into soil and determining which plants and animals live in a region.

Disasters
Occasionally, major disasters change landscapes overnight. For example, earthquakes, hurricanes or volcanic eruptions can devastate huge areas. A large volcanic eruption can release enormous clouds of ash into the atmosphere which can obscure the Sun and cause temporary climate change.

Windstorm

Rainstorm

Folding

Volcano

Faulting

Plate movement
The Earth's crust is made up of plates which move around relative to one another. Britain, for example, was situated in the tropics 250 million years ago.

--------- Plates   ⇨ Movement

Chapter Two

THE HUMAN IMPACT

Worldwide, landscapes are changing at an alarming rate. Compared to the creeping pace at which the forces of nature usually operate, humans can produce dramatic changes very rapidly. This has been particularly true since the beginning of the Industrial Revolution some 250 years ago. In this time the population has soared and technological improvements have led us to manipulate our surroundings more effectively than ever. There is not necessarily anything wrong with humans altering a landscape, as long as the area remains capable of supporting a healthy variety of living things well into the future. Unfortunately, the environment is being damaged and the pace of change is often too rapid for living things to adapt.

The knock-on effect

Any action can produce a whole series of unexpected side effects – or knock-on effects. These often produce far more serious changes than foreseen. For example, one might imagine that the result of felling a forest would be simply to create a treeless area. In fact, cutting trees may harm the soil which then becomes less able to support new vegetation. A substantial decrease in the number of trees growing in an area might even lead to decreased rainfall. Less rainfall makes it harder for plants to grow and dries out the soil, making it more prone to erosion. Such interactions show that by changing one factor, humans can affect many others. Often it is knock-on effects which have been behind the most damaging changes inflicted on the landscape. In the extreme, humans may move into a lush forest and leave it a barren wasteland a few decades later.

△ Even walking can damage the land.

Taking responsibility

The most serious landscape changes are often the combined effect of many people's actions. Most people carry out their own business, forgetting that individual activities added together can cause enormous change. People do not always recognise their contribution to environmental problems. It is easy, for example, to blame farmers for creating huge fields prone to erosion. But stocking our supermarket shelves with cheap and abundant produce usually depends on the farming methods that cause the damage.

The hillwalker syndrome

One would imagine that few activities could be as harmless as walking in the hills. However, in many places, hillwalkers are damaging the environment. Two feet trampling over heather will do no harm. Ten hundred or ten thousand pairs of heavy

boots, on the other hand, will soon march their way through vegetation and soil, leaving a deep scar across beautiful mountain scenery. In almost every activity we do, we are "hillwalking". One family that clears a small patch for cultivation will not damage the forest in which they live. But one million families will soon destroy the forest altogether. Yet each individual family will not perceive the problem as their own since their contribution to the damage seems so small.

Consumption and population

Families have been surviving without irreversibly damaging the environment for thousands of years. Why, then, are we suddenly seeing the rapid destruction of landscapes around us? Two factors underlie the acceleration of the human impact. First, many people, in particular those in wealthy regions like North America and Europe, consume more products which are made from materials taken from the Earth. Also, they have exploited resources from around the world in order to make these products. Secondly, the world's population is continually increasing. Expanding populations will accelerate the impact on landscapes as they build homes and industries, grow food and so on.

Improving technology

People's mobility has greatly improved with the development of air, rail, road and rapid sea transport. Only two hundred years ago, most people never travelled more than a

Growth of cities
In 1940 one in eight people lived in a town or city; today the number is about one in three. Mexico City's population could reach 26.3 million by the year 2000.

few miles beyond their homes. Now many people, particularly in the more wealthy nations, are able to travel hundreds of miles and spend holidays in far-off places. Imagine how a hillside is damaged if walkers trade their boots for motorbikes. This is now common practice in many areas. A few hundred years ago, the railway had not been invented, and the car was a science-fiction dream. Walking was the dominant form of transport. Today, walking has been replaced by automobiles; technology has made a great impact.

The birth of agriculture

Hunter-gatherer communities live by harvesting wild plants and roots and by trapping and hunting wild animals. Thousands of years ago, all people lived in this way; now only a few isolated communities, such as the Bushmen of the Kalahari Desert in southern Africa, live as hunter-gatherers. Since the natural environment provides them with everything they need, these people could not survive if they destroyed the landscape in which they live. However, hunting-gathering requires a large area in which the community can hunt and gather enough wild crops to last them throughout the year. Only a very small population can be sustained in this way.

As human society developed, food production began to change. About 6000 BC, people developed agriculture. They started to tame wild animals and plants, and gradually began to form permanent settlements. These changes marked the beginning of human manipulation of nature. By planting crops instead of gathering them, people could control food production and could make the land support far larger human populations. Agriculture lies at the foundation of human success, but it has also been the main cause

△ Bushmen in southern Africa use their knowledge of their surroundings when they hunt.

of the environmental damage we have caused. About 10 per cent of the world's land surface is currently being cultivated and a further 25 per cent is devoted to the grazing of cattle, sheep and goats. Activities on this enormous scale can hardly fail to affect landscapes around the world.

The growth of agriculture
In its early stages, agriculture had a minimal impact on the environment. Small areas of flat and fertile land were cleared of wild vegetation and planted with crops. Gradually, as the best available areas were used and as human populations swelled, croplands were developed on hillsides, where terraces were sometimes built to control erosion. In some areas, where water was scarce, complex irrigation systems were constructed to convert dry land into productive farmland. As farming increased to keep up with the growing population, the wilderness was pushed back into more marginal and remote areas. Previously arid landscapes grew lush, and fertile areas were ploughed into fields.

As long as the population was small and the soil was kept healthy and the size of herds and flocks was limited, most of these changes were sustainable; they did not affect the ability of the land to produce food in future years. Civilization could continue to develop because it had plenty of food. As populations grew, crop and grazing lands expanded. Today there are so many people in the world that there is intense pressure to increase agricultural productivity in order to grow enough food to feed us all. There are, however, few new frontiers left for agriculture to expand into. Almost all the most productive land is already being used. This is a recipe for disaster. When farmers struggle to plough land not suitable for cropping and to increase the yields on land already planted, this causes many other environmental problems.

Soil erosion
Topsoil is the nutrient-rich surface layer of soil on which plants depend for healthy growth. The loss of just a few centimetres of topsoil can take nature centuries to replace. Yet because of poor farming methods which strip plants off the land, exposing soil to wind and rain, billions of tonnes of topsoil are eroded from fields around the world every year. As topsoil is washed or blown away, the soil's fertility decreases, and eventually agriculture in the area may have to be abandoned.

Many hilly countries in particular have suffered from the effects of soil erosion. In Nepal, for example, where population pressures have led to the need for more cropland for growing food and more firewood for heating and cooking, the vast forests that covered its mountain slopes just a few decades ago are disappearing. Once

△ Wind can carry away exposed topsoil which is vital for growing crops.

△ Erosion on this hillside in Spain has left a barren slope.

the protection of the trees and other plants which hold together the soil is gone, rain rapidly washes soil from the slopes into the great rivers which flow to India and Bangladesh. The situation is so serious that soil has been described as Nepal's "most precious export", an export for which it gets no gains, only losses. The changes to Nepal's landscape have been devastating. The barren and eroded landscape created by cutting down forests is not only less attractive, but also much less productive. The ecology of these mountains, which has been evolving for 50 million years, is being damaged by population pressures, under-mining the land's potential to produce food.

Nepal is not alone. Around the world, previously lush landscapes are turning into semi-deserts as a result of soil loss. In Ethiopia, millions of people struggling for survival have already destroyed most of their forests. As they farm eroded land for a living, the problem gets worse. The Ethiopian highlands lose an estimated one billion tonnes of topsoil every year.

Fertilizers

Erosion is not only a problem in developing nations. For example, the United States has considerable soil-loss problems. On the Great Plains of the midwest, where huge herds of buffalo once lived, there now exist treeless fields stretching in all directions as far as the eye can see. These are a product of years of farming. The bare fields are prone to erosion and the damage being caused is extremely serious. It is estimated that the United States loses some five billion tonnes of topsoil every year – about eight times more than is produced by nature. Farmers, however, are obscuring visible damage by using fertilizers, which help crops grow. At great cost, huge quantities of these artificial nutrients are scattered over the fields, not only to replace the nutrients absorbed by the last year's crop, but also to replace those washed away with the topsoil.

Rainforest destruction

In tropical rainforests, which lie around the Equator, most nutrients are stored in vegetation rather than in the soil. These forests thrive by taking in the nutrients from organic waste such as dead leaves, which quickly decay in the hot, damp conditions. When dead plants and leaves rot, they become part of the soil and their nutrients are absorbed by growing plants. When the forests are cut down, the soil loses its fertility because there is no rotting vegetation. Rainforests, which have the most plentiful and varied wildlife in the world, become infertile deserts in this way. This process is now happening throughout the tropics, particularly in southeast Asia and Brazil, where vast areas of forest are felled every year for ranching, timber and farming. The farmers that move in after the forest is cleared all too often discover that the soil is too poor for productive farming. Every year an area the size of England, Scotland and Wales is transformed from lush and densely wooded landscape into poor scrubland capable of supporting only a handful of cattle.

However, it is possible for people to use the rainforests in non-destructive ways. The forests contain a wealth of woods, bark, fruit, potential medicines and other things that can be harvested. Furthermore, for centuries, people living in the forest have used shifting agriculture without damaging the rainforest. Shifting agriculture is a type of farming in which small clearings are made and crops planted in them. After a few years, when the soil begins to lose its fertility, the clearing is abandoned and the forest allowed to grow back for 20-25 years. For generations, people using this method have reaped the benefits from their environment without damaging it.

Unfortunately, population growth and poverty are forcing these practices to be abandoned. The countries in which rainforests lie are usually very poor. The growing population is forced to recultivate the forest clearings before they have had time to regenerate. The forest becomes pockmarked with barren areas. The changing landscape vividly illustrates the destruction of the forest and the soil, on which people depend for growing crops. Eventually forests will remain only on slopes too steep to farm. This process has already occurred in some areas of the world. In Madagascar, for example, the landscape has changed drastically in the past decades from being very thickly forested to having almost no forest left at all.

△ Nearly five million hectares of rainforest were burned in Amazonia in 1988, making many species extinct. In addition, during this century 90 Amazonian tribes disappeared.

Flooding

Deforestation and erosion can lead to disastrous floods. Forests help soil absorb rainfall by breaking the fall of the rain with branches and leaves and helping the rain which drips through the canopy to soak into the soil through the network of roots. When forest cover is stripped away, rain washes along the ground instead of soaking into its surface. The water from heavy rains drains into rivers very rapidly, causing downstream flooding. In this way, many of the recent, devastating floods in places like Bangladesh are directly linked to the rainfall on the deforested Himalayan slopes. Furthermore, the soil washed by the rain from these treeless slopes settles in the slow-moving lowland rivers, blocking the river's flow and increasing the risk of flooding. The huge sheets of water that stretch for miles across countries like Bangladesh during floods may only be temporary changes in a landscape, but they cause many deaths and leave behind lasting damage to homes and crops.

Livestock damage
The increasing number of people has led to growing livestock populations which also put pressure on landscapes. There are now over three billion cows, sheep and goats, and together they depend on an area more than double that used for growing crops. In many places, herds and flocks are far larger than the land can cope with, as the vegetation is stripped away faster than it can grow back. For example, in areas of the Middle East, where there are several times more animals than the land can support, serious deterioration is taking place. When the pasture has been so overgrazed that it can no longer support flocks of sheep, the goats and camels move in. Eventually, the damage will become so severe that the land may be unable to supply even these animals with food, and the terrain may turn from scrub and grassland to semi-desert. This is called desertification. Overpopulation by humans and animals is one of the main

△ Overgrazing can turn a fertile area to desert.

reasons why deserts around the world are expanding. In Africa, for example, the Sahara Desert is growing in all directions, leaving people without land to farm or raise animals. Desertification is also occurring where deserts did not previously exist.

Landscape changes caused by herds of livestock are by no means a new phenomenon. In many of the hilly areas of Britain, for example, the introduction of sheep had a significant impact on the creation of today's landscape. Many areas now covered by moorland were once forested. As demand for timber for firewood and building grew, these woods were felled. Sheep prevented the forests from growing back by eating the shoots of young trees, thus playing a critical role in

△ The Aral Sea in the Soviet Union has shrunk to nearly half its size.

transforming the landscape. Today, many islands in lakes, inaccessible to sheep, retain the diverse trees and plants which once covered the surrounding moorland.

Problems with irrigation

Problems can arise even in places where people attempt to improve the environment, by irrigating parched lands to grow crops, for example. For a few years, irrigation may make a dry area bloom. However, in places where water has not drained from the soil properly, irrigation leads to the soil becoming too wet for plants to grow. Also, salts build up in the soil when the water evaporates. The vast, white expanses created in this way are incapable of supporting any plantlife. The problem is particularly acute in areas like Pakistan and Iraq. Ironically, therefore, poor cropland can actually be damaged by irrigation and instead of producing a lush landscape it can lead to the creation of new deserts.

Human activities have had other effects on natural water sources. In some places, water diverted from rivers to feed huge irrigation schemes or to provide water for urban populations has had an enormous impact on the environment. In the Soviet Union, the immense, inland Aral Sea has been reduced by 40 per cent. At the present rate it could disappear in about 30 years. The sea was previously fed by a number of large rivers, most of whose water is now used for irrigation, so it is no longer being filled. The Aral Sea is simply evaporating, threatening serious ecological and climatic damage to the region.

Cities and towns

Agriculture is only one way in which people are changing the landscape. The modern industrial society, in which industry supplies more jobs than agriculture, has resulted in the building of many structures, like dams, factories and so on. One small house tucked inside a forest will have little effect on the overall landscape, but a clustering of many homes has a big impact. It is difficult to imagine that the urban landscapes we have created have replaced green fields, forests and meadows. Concrete now covers large areas of land. Cities like London, Los Angeles, Tokyo and Djakarta in Indonesia sprawl out for miles.

Villages, towns and cities generally began at the core of fertile areas because people could grow food nearby. These farms then fed the population of the settlements. But as cities expand, more agricultural land is covered over. In this way, millions of hectares of prime farmland around the world are being lost. In much of the poorer world in recent years, cities and towns have grown explosively as people escaping rural poverty have flocked to them. Already large population centres like Mexico City, Lagos in Nigeria and Bombay in India are still growing at alarming rates.

In the countryside as well, population growth has led to a need for more homes and the area covered by housing has increased. Most of these houses are built on land good for growing food. Worldwide, there is an increasing conflict between the need for land to build on and the need for land to farm.

Other structures
It is not only housing that covers a growing area of the world's surface; we build many other structures too. Today we marvel at many of the monuments built by our ancestors, who did not have the help of modern technology. Landmarks like the pyramids of Egypt and the Great Wall of China can hardly fail to affect the landscape – in fact the Great Wall is even visible to the naked eye from space. However, these ancient constructions are few and far between. Now we regularly build thousands of huge structures. Dotted around our landscapes are factories, power stations and large dams. The countryside is criss-crossed by a growing network of roads, and miles of concrete and tarmac stretching over land once covered in plantlife. Few landscapes in the Western world have escaped the introduction of thousands of power cables and pylons. Millions of kilometres of cables suspended a few metres above the ground alter the landscape considerably. We also mine vast quantities of minerals like coal and iron. Mining leaves behind gaping holes and artificial hills, prominent features on some modern landscapes.

Dam schemes
Dams can provide clean electricity. However, they can also have a devastating impact on the environment. The Itaipu Dam in Amazonia flooded some 120,000 hectares of forest, displaced 50,000 people and caused the extinction of some rainforest species.

△ Hong Kong was a fishing village 200 years ago.

Pollution

Another major change human activity has caused is less visible than other kinds of landscape alterations: pollution. Spraying chemicals onto fields, discharging waste from factories and releasing the gases from burning fuel pollute the environment. The many forms of pollution can change the landscape in varying ways. Some of the most serious results of pollution threaten our very existence.

Acid rain

Some 100 million tonnes of sulphur dioxide gas are released into the atmosphere every year from burning fossil fuels (coal, oil and gas) in power stations and cars. When this gas reacts in the atmosphere it produces acid rain and other pollutants which damage plants, corrode buildings and can harm human and animal health. All around the world, forests affected by acid rain are dying. In parts of Germany, areas densely forested only a decade ago are now barren.

Only the skeletons of dead trees are left. Acid rain also damages crops, reducing yields significantly. It is estimated that acid rain costs Europe more than $10 billion a year. To make the changes necessary to halve emissions of gases that cause acid rain would cost countries in the European Community at least $5 billion a year until the end of the century.

Global warming

An even more serious effect of pollution, with the potential to cause landscape changes even greater than those we have already experienced, is global warming. Carbon dioxide and other gases naturally trap heat in the atmosphere (known as the Greenhouse Effect). This phenomenon keeps the Earth at a temperature suitable for living things. However, industrial societies depend on vast amounts of fossil fuels to generate energy. As a result of

△ Acid rain has damaged this German forest.

19

burning these fossil fuels, the level of carbon dioxide in the atmosphere is rapidly rising. Most scientists now agree that by increasing the amount of carbon dioxide, humans will cause the Earth's atmosphere to warm. It is predicted that this will cause changes in climates around the world and produce more droughts, floods and hurricanes. Global warming could turn now fertile farming areas like the American midwest into arid regions where little would grow.

If global warming is not stopped and temperatures rise, it is not known how plantlife will adapt. The speed of change may be too rapid for many species to cope with, causing forests to die and crops to wither. It may be impossible to move our staple crops to warmer, wetter regions where the soil and other conditions are suitable. What is certain, however, is that many landscapes around the world will change drastically. As the world warms, experts fear that the sea levels will rise, flooding coastal regions. It is estimated that nearly half a million kilometres of coastline could be submerged and that tens of millions of people could be made homeless.

It is impossible to reduce the amount of carbon dioxide released when fossil fuels are burned, but fossil fuels are vital to our industries and lifestyles. The most realistic way of tackling this problem is simply to burn less coal, oil and gas. International action has to be taken, as many scientists now agree that if greenhouse gases continue to be released at present levels, the climate will change faster in the next century than at any time since the last Ice Age. They believe that by the end of the next century, the world's climate could become hotter than it has been in two million years.

△ Severe storms are expected to become more common as global warming increases.

◁ Snowless winters in the Alps are feared to be a symptom of rising global temperatures.

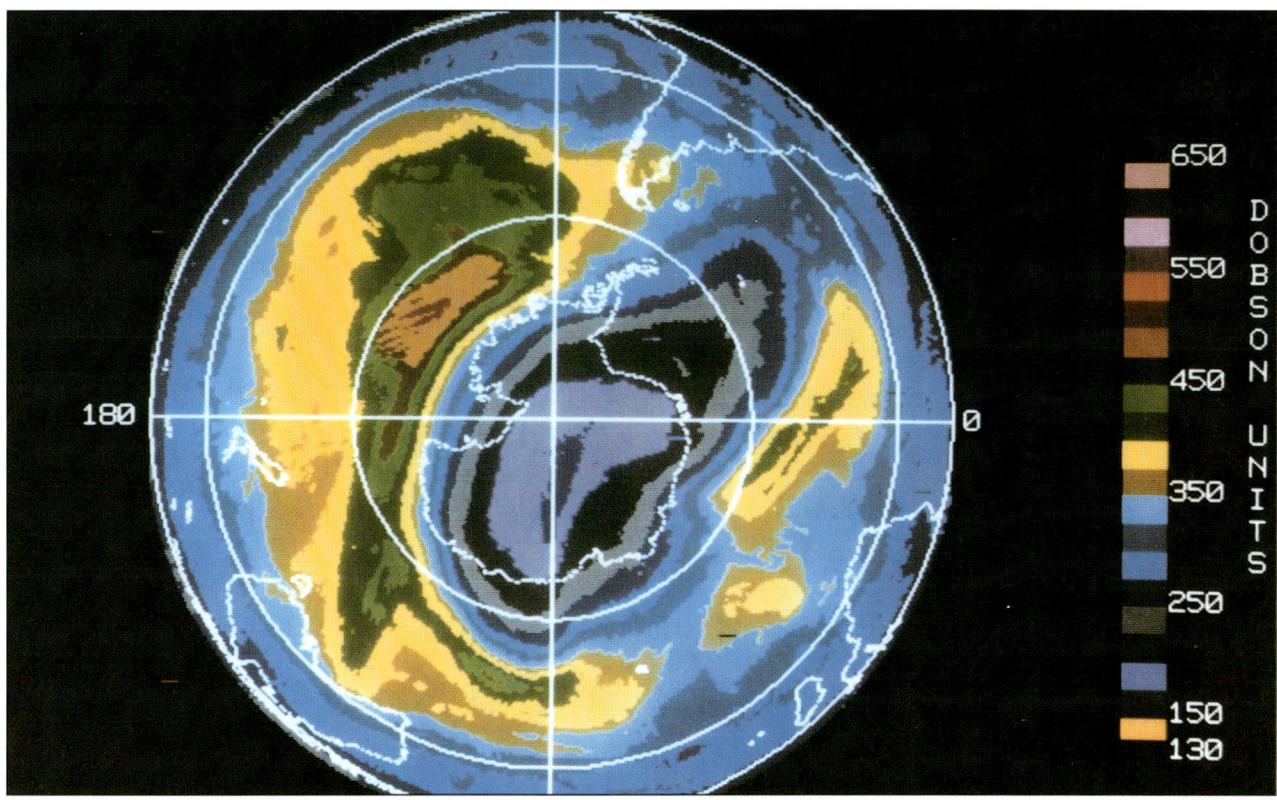

△ A satellite photograph of the hole in the ozone layer

The hole in the ozone layer

Yet another form of pollution threatens the global environment. The release of certain gases is leading to the depletion of the ozone layer. The ozone layer contains ozone gas. It exists in the atmosphere at a height of 15 to 30 kilometres. This layer filters out ultraviolet radiation from the Sun which can cause skin cancer and other damage to living things. A number of human-made chemicals destroy this layer when they get into the atmosphere, most notably CFCs (chlorofluorocarbons), which are used in air conditioners, fridges, foam packaging, insulation and in the electronics industry.

In 1984, a hole in the ozone layer was recorded above Antarctica and now the ozone is thinning above the Arctic. Although scientists cannot foresee with certainty the results of damage to the ozone layer, allowing it to become too depleted could have serious consequences. Plants and animals might be harmed by the increased levels of ultraviolet radiation reaching the Earth's surface and some species could die out altogether. For instance, a large increase in ultraviolet radiation could affect plankton, the tiny organisms in the oceans which form the basis of the food chain. If this occurred, their numbers could drop. This would affect all life in the oceans because many species, including whales, depend on plankton for food. A similar process could take place with land animals or plants – a situation which would have grave consequences on the environment. If we wait to test these predictions, it will probably be too late to reverse the damage.

One step has been taken to decrease the amount of gases released which destroy the ozone layer. In 1987, an international agreement, the Montreal Protocol, was signed by many countries who agreed to stop using the most harmful CFCs. However, many environmentalists believe quicker action is necessary to prevent further damage to the ozone layer.

Pressures on the landscape

Almost every human activity affects the environment. Recently, the speed of change has caused concern. The destruction of the rainforests and the expansion of cities are two of the most noticeable transformations in the last 50 years. However, the most serious damage is from agriculture, and few areas have not been affected by this activity.

Population
The number of people alive is continually and rapidly increasing, but resources and farmland are limited.

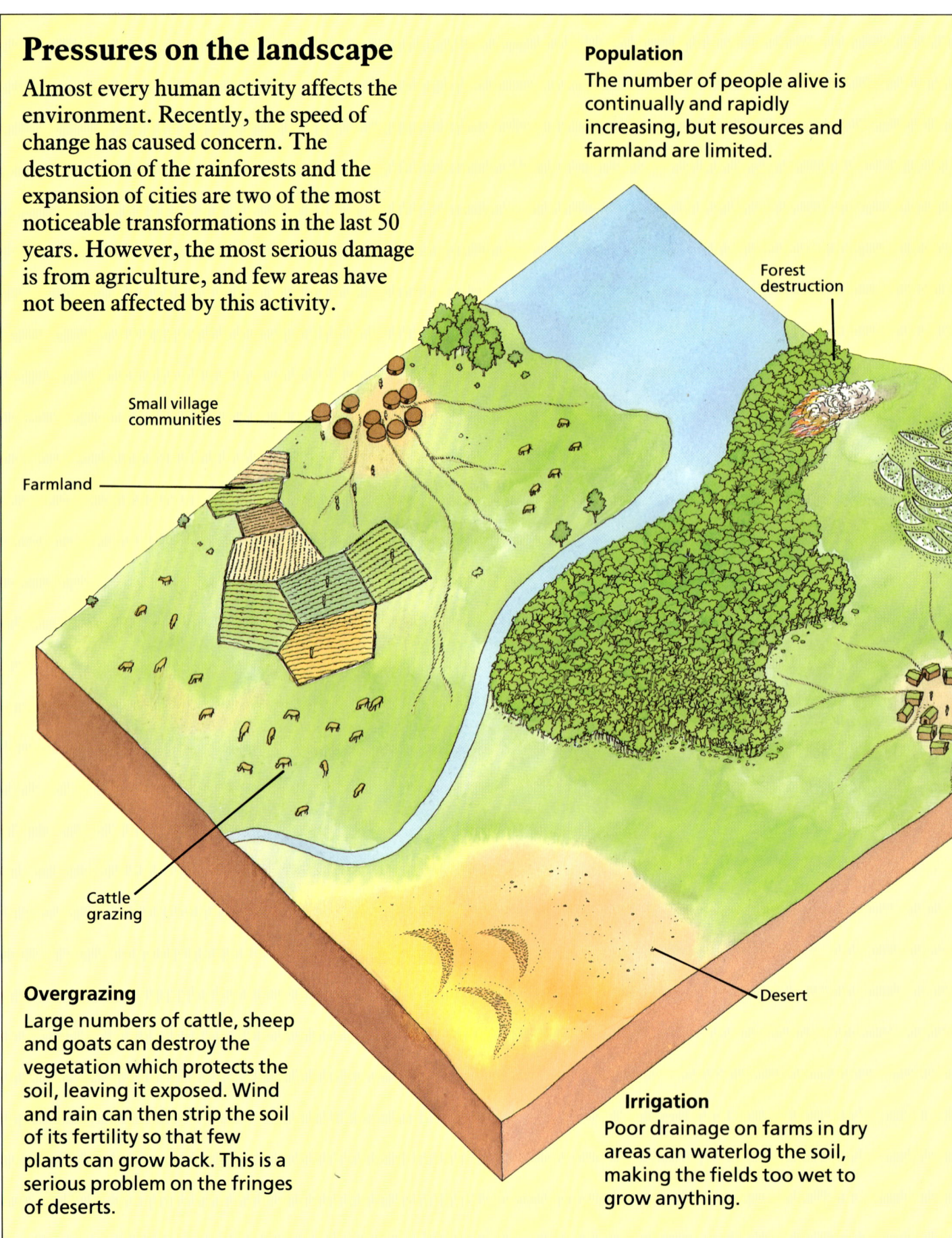

Forest destruction

Small village communities

Farmland

Cattle grazing

Desert

Overgrazing
Large numbers of cattle, sheep and goats can destroy the vegetation which protects the soil, leaving it exposed. Wind and rain can then strip the soil of its fertility so that few plants can grow back. This is a serious problem on the fringes of deserts.

Irrigation
Poor drainage on farms in dry areas can waterlog the soil, making the fields too wet to grow anything.

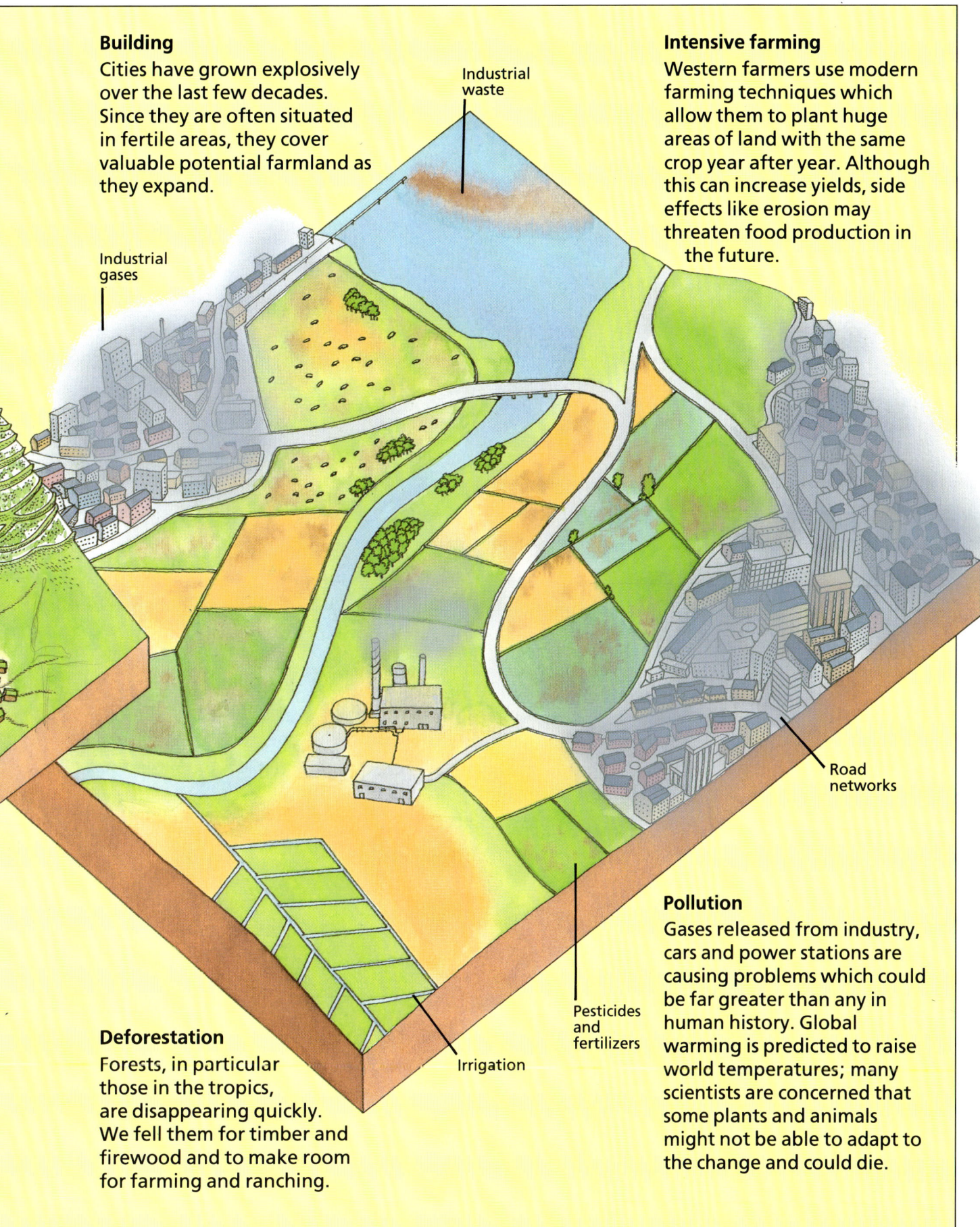

Building

Cities have grown explosively over the last few decades. Since they are often situated in fertile areas, they cover valuable potential farmland as they expand.

Industrial gases

Industrial waste

Intensive farming

Western farmers use modern farming techniques which allow them to plant huge areas of land with the same crop year after year. Although this can increase yields, side effects like erosion may threaten food production in the future.

Road networks

Deforestation

Forests, in particular those in the tropics, are disappearing quickly. We fell them for timber and firewood and to make room for farming and ranching.

Irrigation

Pesticides and fertilizers

Pollution

Gases released from industry, cars and power stations are causing problems which could be far greater than any in human history. Global warming is predicted to raise world temperatures; many scientists are concerned that some plants and animals might not be able to adapt to the change and could die.

23

Chapter Three

LEARNING FROM THE PAST

People are often reluctant to accept that things could go seriously wrong in the near future. Those who voice concern are labelled as scaremongers, and many people are quick to point out that we have always muddled through in the past. This is actually far from the truth. Some archaeologists believe that environmental damage, recorded by changing landscapes, has almost certainly contributed to the downfall of some major civilizations in the past. We cannot be certain that technology will be able to protect us from the damage that we are currently inflicting on our surroundings. Human society has made it to this point by learning from past mistakes and adapting its actions accordingly. This is the task we face today.

Ancient Greece

Plato, a great Greek philosopher who lived in 400 BC, has left us a vivid idea of the damage that humans were already imposing on their environment some 2,400 years ago. Writing about his native Greece, he states, "Long ago, the soil far surpassed all others and its yield was most copious... The soil was the best in the world, water was abundant and the climates temperate. But in the succeeding years, torrential rains carried the soils from the high levels off to the depths of the sea. What remains is like a body wasted by disease, for with the rich, friable soil washed away, only a skeleton of the land is left. Before this happened, the high hills were covered with soil and trees. But now, some of the mountains can afford sustenance only for bees. In the older times, the mountain provided unlimited fodder for cattle, but the trees were felled for huge buildings... Before the land became barren,

◁ The Acropolis in Athens stands as a monument to the sophistication of Ancient Greece. But damage to the environment limited the civilization's success.

The Roman Empire

The Roman Empire (500 BC – 500 AD) suffered from similar problems. The Romans destroyed their forests for farmland, firewood and timber, causing erosion which in turn led to rivers being blocked by silt. Fields gradually turned into marshes – a perfect breeding ground for mosquitoes which brought malaria to Rome. The Roman Empire lasted longer than that of Greece, possibly because its armies were stronger and could make sure that a steady supply of food from the provinces reached the capital. However, despite the strength of their army, the Romans could not depend on far-off places indefinitely. Productive areas of North Africa, which provided the Romans with much of their grain, were placed under more and more stress and eventually they too lost their fertility. Today, more than 2,000 years later, the Italian slopes and North African lands have not yet fully recovered from the pressures put on them by Roman agriculture.

Downfall of the Sumerians

Ecological disasters serious enough to contribute to the downfall of societies are recorded even earlier than the problems described by Plato. The Sumerian civilization that existed on the banks of the Tigris and Euphrates rivers, in what is now Iraq, was at its height some 4,000 years ago. The Sumerians developed the earliest known civilization. They built extraordinary monuments and invented the written word. Although the area in which they lived was extremely dry, the broad flood plains of the Tigris and Euphrates were fertile when irrigated. The rivers

the soil benefited from the yearly rain. A plentiful supply of water was received and stored in the soil… Now the water runs off the barren ground into the sea."

Plato was not alone in expressing concern. A few centuries before, others had argued that crops should not be planted on slopes, as farming would lead to erosion. In the end, this opinion was put aside as population pressures prevailed, and the slopes were farmed for as long as enough fertile soil remained to support the crops. Plato's account indicates that long before Greece had entered the height of its civilization, human activity had already created serious local environmental problems. These problems led to Greece's dependence on areas further away for their food. It seems likely that damage to the environment undermined their self-sufficiency in food and eventually diminished the success of the civilization.

provided enough water to convert the barren deserts into productive fields.

Archaeologists have calculated that at the height of the civilization, Sumerian yields of grain compared with those of fertile Western wheatfields today. Farmers were able to produce large surpluses of food and this allowed the population to grow and huge cities to be built. Ur, the largest of these, is estimated to have had a population of about 300,000 during its peak. The people manipulated the landscape to improve their living conditions: by building extensive irrigation projects, for example. In this way the Sumerian civilization blossomed for over a thousand years.

But gradually, as the hot sun evaporated the water from the irrigated fields, salt built up in the soil. Eventually the soil became less capable of supporting crops, and later, unfit for farming altogether. By 1700 BC, the great Sumerian cities had declined because of lack of food, and became either abandoned or impoverished villages. This is the first known example of a human

population experiencing a major ecological disaster. The civilization's population had simply placed too much demand on the environment and, as a result, the landscape slowly transformed as great buildings disappeared under desert sands.

Another ancient civilization that suffered because of its impact on the environment existed in the Indus Valley, in what is now Pakistan, around 2500 BC. Little is known about the reasons for its decline, but experts believe that it is probable that the huge forests which existed along the river banks were gradually felled for firewood and to make room for agriculture. The erosion and floods that followed devastated the society.

The Mayans' decline
On the other side of the world, in Central America, it is likely that similar stresses caused the downfall of the Mayan civilization. Between 500 BC and 900 AD, this civilization flourished, expanding over what are now the lowlands of Guatemala. The population continued to grow until it

△ These pyramids in Mexico were part of the Mayan Empire.

reached about five million people.

Sediments recovered from the bottom of lakes near the Mayan ruins show that overuse of the soil was causing the Mayan fields to erode seriously. This destroyed the area's fertility and contributed to the civilization's collapse.

Modern problems

Today, the environmental predicament we face is as serious as that of the dawn of civilization on the banks of the Euphrates. However, there are major differences between today's situation and the one that existed then. On the dark side, during the last 5,000 years, the world's population has grown from some 100 million to over five billion. The pressures the Sumerians and Mayans placed on the environment were restricted to specific areas of the world. Today's enormous and growing population is damaging environments worldwide, and this stress is reflected in the transformation of landscapes on all continents. However, our modern civilization has far more

understanding of the problems we are creating. The technologies which have developed may help us control the damage. Perhaps now we can stop the cycle of destruction experienced by past civilizations.

Changing landscapes in the United States

Settlers in North America arrived in one of the richest environments on Earth. As they moved westwards, swathes of forests were cut for building and farming, and prairies were ploughed. The settlers began to transform the landscape, treating the land's resources as though they were inexhaustible. Today the same mentality exists. The expansion of cities and towns swallows millions of hectares of agricultural land every year. Furthermore, the methods of agriculture employed are causing considerable damage. Around 100 million hectares of land are currently turning to unproductive desert and a third of the irrigated cropland in the western states is showing signs of salting. Erosion is removing soil from 40 million hectares of farmland, and almost 10 per cent of this land is already damaged beyond repair.

If climatic factors like global warming aggravate the problems in the United States by causing more droughts or severe storms, the world's food supplies could be threatened. During the 1980s, the United States exported 120 million tonnes of grain to the rest of the world. If food supplies become scarce this could cause worldwide economic, social and political instability. We can learn from civilizations of the past which suffered from their mistakes. We ought to take more notice of the changes now occurring in our landscapes. They may be warning us of impending crises.

◁ The United States has huge stores of grain that can be used in times of shortage, but repeated droughts have depleted stocks.

Chapter Four

CHANGING OUR PRIORITIES

One of the major factors that led to the downfall of the Mayan, Sumerian and Indus civilizations was the destruction of the fertility of their lands because of their farming methods. Without productive lands which gave them a plentiful supply of food, the stability that allowed these civilizations to exist was lost and their demise became inevitable. It seems sensible, therefore, that we review our own farming practices, our consumption of resources and the size of our population before it is too late. We do have means at our disposal that could help us reverse some of the problems we have created. For example, by emphasising organic farming in areas where food is plentiful, we can minimise our dependence on chemicals and other harmful farming practices.

Modern farming

Worldwide, people have changed their farming techniques dramatically since the beginning of the century. When people first began to cultivate the land, they used shifting agriculture, like many successful rainforest farmers still do today. They planted crops for a few years before moving on to other patches, thereby allowing the soil to regain nutrients from the wild plants which grew back over it. This is known as letting the land lie fallow, or untilled: a practice which dominated agriculture until the 19th century.

In the 19th century, farmers discovered that by planting a field with a different crop each year and by choosing crops which release nutrients back into the soil that the previous year's crop had removed, land could be kept in continuous use. It was not long after this that scientists invented pesticides and fertilizers, chemicals which could help produce larger yields.

The basis for today's agricultural practices were in place. It became possible

◁ This view of an intensively farmed landscape shows some of the negative side effects of modern agriculture: exposed soil and lack of hedgerows lead to erosion, and one-crop farming can make soil infertile. We need to adopt methods of producing food which are sustainable if we are to survive into the future.

to farm an area year in, year out with one crop, replenishing lost nutrients with artificial fertilizers. This method of farming often encourages pests because it kills off their natural predators, so farmers began to apply vast quantities of pesticides to control pests. Often supported by huge government subsidies, farming changed from being an activity that involved the subtle manipulation of nature, to one in which sophisticated technology is used to squeeze out more food from nature.

Landscapes under pressure

As agriculture expanded, hedgerows and trees were ripped up as fields became larger – a process which continues today. Meadows that once supported hundreds of species of wild plants were ploughed and planted with only one crop. Areas that used to support many different crops became grain deserts, with one species dominating the landscape. With their natural habitats destroyed, the number of birds and animals decreased alarmingly.

However, there is no doubt that yields have increased dramatically as farming methods have developed. This is often used as evidence that these new farming methods are highly efficient. However, we should remember that what is most important is the ability of the land to support the plant and animal life that depend on it – not only now but well into the future. The evidence so far suggests that modern farming practices will not be able to sustain productivity and could wipe out many species of wildlife and seriously damage the environment.

By enthusiastically adopting modern farming techniques, the wealthier nations are steadily impoverishing their farmland. Large, treeless fields are prone to erosion, and although we may temporarily replace lost fertility with fertilizers, topsoil is essential to farming and is often not being produced at the rate it is being depleted. Another problem is that the pesticides we spray on fields get into our food and water, and pests become increasingly immune to them. The creatures which naturally control pests, like birds and spiders, are rapidly disappearing because of pesticide poisoning or because their natural habitat has been destroyed.

Energy-intensive farming

Modern agriculture uses fleets of tractors and other machines which need a vast amount of energy to run. Pesticides and fertilizers also use a lot of energy in their manufacture. It takes approximately one tonne of oil to provide the energy to make one tonne of nitrogen fertilizer. During the period 1950 to 1983, the average consumption of these fertilizers rose from five kilograms to 25 kilograms per year for every inhabitant of the planet. This means that over 100 million tonnes of oil are used every year simply to produce the fertilizers modern agriculture demands.

This consumption cannot continue into the future because fossil fuel reserves are running low. Also, burning oil in farm machines produces carbon dioxide, which could contribute to global warming. Ironically, as modern farming erodes soil and destroys nature's balance, more fertilizers will be needed and more energy will have to be provided in order to produce the same amount of food. The need to change our approach is increasingly pressing. We must bring back the diversity that previously existed in our environment and let nature, and not oil, provide most of the energy we need to grow our food.

The organic option

One of the ways in which we can begin to reverse the negative effects of modern farming is by supporting the organic option. Instead of artificial fertilizers and pesticides, organic farmers rely on crop rotation and manure to maintain the soil's fertility. They apply no artificial chemicals to their land. To combat pests, they keep

△ The praying mantis is a natural pest control.

hedgerows and encourage a wide mix of species on their land, making use of natural predators to keep pest populations down. Organic farming is becoming increasingly widespread and could be a major step in rejuvenating landscapes, although one drawback is that it often produces lower yields than intensive farming, which makes it less attractive to poor countries.

Farming in developing countries

Problems associated with modern farming techniques do not only affect the industrialised world. Many developing countries are facing even greater problems as a result of harmful farming methods. Each area has a different problem so it is difficult to generalise about them, but often Western influence is the cause. In parts of Africa, for example, prior to Western interference, a complex relationship existed between herders and farmers living in areas where persistent droughts made farming difficult. The farmers occupied the best land and exchanged some of their crops, mainly sorghum and millet, for meat and milk produced by the nomadic herders. These herders lived on more marginal land and kept moving so that their cattle did not completely eliminate the sparse vegetation on which they grazed. For centuries, small populations of farmers and herders lived successfully in these areas.

Cash crops

When Westerners arrived they introduced cash crops – crops grown for export value instead of for food. They often took the best land, forcing the native farmers to move to poorer areas and pushing the herders into the fringes of the desert. The herders could no longer move freely, and their herds overgrazed vulnerable lands. As a consequence, the desert expanded. The relationship between herder and farmer also disintegrated because, as they scratched a living from poorer lands, neither could produce enough food to exchange.

△ Tea is grown in Tanzania as a cash crop – this land does not provide food for local people.

△ China's attempts to control the population explosion have slowed the rate of growth, but not by enough.

▷ In Europe, population growth is low but the population density is already very high.

▷▷ Increasing numbers of people and the growth of industries to provide goods for them result in further scarring of landscapes in the search for resources.

When famines began to occur regularly in these areas, the Western industrialised countries tried to help. All too often, they simply introduced the farming methods they were familiar with. These can cause even more damage in Africa than they cause in the West. Western advisors often tend to ignore the complex systems that the African farmers have developed over the centuries. Native farming methods do not require expensive fertilizers or irrigation schemes but depend on farming in a sustainable way, working with the environment rather than taking the more short-sighted and costly Western approach.

The population explosion

Expansion of agriculture increases damage to landscapes. Population growth has made it necessary for farmers to produce more from their lands – the same factor that caused the downfall of the Sumerian, Indus, Greek, Roman and Mayan civilizations. It is ironic that the very success of these societies contributed to

their decline. By evolving sophisticated social and economic structures, they were able to produce the agricultural surpluses necessary to support large cities whose inhabitants enjoyed far higher standards of living than less organised peoples living elsewhere. But as populations grew, more food was required to feed the people, so farmers were urged to put excessive pressure on their land. Eventually, the system could yield no more, the land suffered, harvests began to decline and the societies collapsed. Today, our society faces a similar fate. All the advances we have made are useless unless we are able to grow food for ourselves.

Controlling population growth

Population pressures are central to many cases of environmental damage and landscape change. We are currently undergoing an unprecedented population explosion. At the present growth rate, the number of people in the world will double by the year 2030. Doubling the existing

number of people on the planet will place unbearable stress on the environment.

The record of controlling population increase has not been good and most attempts have had little impact so far. In theory, humans can curb population growth by using the many existing forms of birth control. Unfortunately, however, few issues are affected as much by the "hillwalker syndrome" as birth control. Most people perceive their actions as individual, thus insignificant, although all actions added together can have an enormous effect. Many families, especially in areas where education is poor, do not realise there is a need for population control. Education, therefore, will be crucial to the success of future population programmes. A more difficult problem is that in poor regions, families rely on their members to bring in income. Also, if there is a high mortality rate, mothers will have more children in case they do not all survive. Thus, if health care and living standards improve, birth rates are likely to go down.

Population control is a sensitive issue. Some people are against contraception on moral or religious grounds, which is one reason why the issue has not always been given the attention it deserves. But the fact that the world population could double in the next 40 years means that there is now no time to lose.

Controlling resource use
The exploitation of mineral and energy resources also needs to be controlled. We have to reduce the amount of fertile agricultural land lost by the expansion of cities and the building of roads, dams and so on. Sensible planning would help. Cities should be designed to be more compact, and more efficient public transport systems would lessen reliance on fossil fuels and reduce the need for more road building. Resource use also needs to be controlled because vast amounts of energy are required by the factories which convert raw materials into the products we consume in huge quantities. Renewable resources, which

regenerate themselves, like wind and water, could potentially provide much of our energy in the future. At present, most of this energy comes from fossil fuels, which will eventually run out.

Furthermore, in view of the fact that carbon dioxide is the main contributor to global warming, we must make reducing emissions of this gas an urgent priority. Currently, we burn vast amounts of fossil fuels to generate electricity, to run our cars and to power our factories. The technology exists to harness the energy from the Sun, wind and water power, sources of energy which do not contribute to global warming. Unfortunately though, we have left it so late that global warming will get worse before we can significantly reduce our fossil fuel consumption by using alternative energy. Experts have calculated that energy efficiency measures could substantially reduce energy needs. This would be a step in the right direction, but even this is not enough to make the necessary reduction if catastrophic global warming is to be avoided. To reverse the possibility of global warming, countries must co-operate to cut the amount of carbon dioxide released as soon as possible. At the moment the levels are still rising.

If human society is to survive we will have to take more notice of the changes happening around us. During the last century, humans have made many advances, but the rate of change has been so rapid that we have impoverished many of the world's richest landscapes, a clear signal that we are causing serious damage to the environment. We depend on nature and on the food it provides us for our very survival. In the short run, we may be able to bypass nature by spraying chemical fertilizers and scattering pesticides over our fields. In the long run, this will cause many damaging side effects which will force us to change our practices. Soon we must acknowledge that we rely on a healthy environment for our food. Controlling the population explosion, minimising our resource use and reviewing our farming practices are challenges that we must all face up to if we are to avoid a major global disaster.

△ This wind farm in California is an example of the potential for energy production in the future.

GLOSSARY

acid rain the result of sulphur dioxide and nitrogen oxides reacting with other gases in the atmosphere. This produces dilute solutions of acid which fall as rain.

CFCs (chlorofluorocarbons) chemicals used in air conditioners, fridges, some foam packaging, insulation and the electronics industry, which damage the ozone layer.

continental drift the term which describes how the Earth's crust continually changes as it moves across a layer of partially molten rock some 50 km below the Earth's surface.

developing countries countries with little industry and mainly rural economies. Average incomes are generally far lower than in the industrialised nations, and health and education provision is often poor.

ecology living things and their habitat.

fertilizer substance containing chemicals necessary for healthy plant growth. It is used to compensate for poor soil or soil depleted by repeated cropping.

fossil fuel the fossilised remains of plants and organisms, which can be burned for energy. Coal, gas and oil are all fossil fuels.

geology the study of the different types of rocks and how they were formed.

Greenhouse Effect the natural process by which certain gases in the Earth's atmosphere trap heat from the Sun. Human activities have increased the amounts of these gases, threatening to trap more heat, which could lead to a rise in temperatures – known as global warming.

industrialised countries countries with economies based around industry; factories provide more jobs than agriculture. Compared to developing countries, income per head is generally high.

Industrial Revolution the development of manufacturing industries and a rapid escalation of resource use. It began in Britain in the 18th century and quickly spread across Europe and North America.

intensive farming planting huge areas of land with one crop year after year, and using aids like irrigation, pesticides and fertilizers in order to increase productivity.

knock-on effect an unexpected effect from an action.

organic produce food grown on land which has had no artificial fertilizers or pesticides applied for at least two years.

ozone layer a layer which exists in the atmosphere at a height of between 15 and 30 km. It contains a high level of ozone which filters out harmful radiation from the Sun. Some gases released by human activities have created a hole in the ozone layer.

pesticide substance used to control pests. The three main types are herbicides, fungicides and insecticides, which are designed to kill weeds, fungi and insects.

renewable resource resources that regenerate themselves (for example, wind, wood and fish) as opposed to non-renewable resources which can only be extracted once (like metals).

shifting agriculture a type of farming in which small clearings are made for crops. After a few years the forest is allowed to grow back over the clearing and the soil recovers in this way.

sustainable society a society which uses resources in such a way that it can continue to support the current lifestyle of its population indefinitely.

topography the features of a landscape.

INDEX

acid rain 19, 35
agriculture 12-15, 18, 22, 23, 25-33
ancient Greece 24, 25
Aral Sea 17

Bangladesh 16
Brazil 15
Bushmen 12

carbon dioxide 19, 20, 34
cash crops 31, 33
CFCs 21, 35
China 32
Chipco movement 30
cities 11, 17-18, 22-23, 32
climate 3, 5-9, 17, 20, 27
consumption 11, 22, 34
continental drift 6, 35
crop rotation 28

dams 18
deforestation 15, 23
desertification 16, 20
disasters 9
drought 27

energy 34
energy-intensive farming 30
Ethiopia 14

famine 32
fertility 13, 15, 16, 25, 26, 28, 29
fertilizers 14, 28, 29, 30, 32, 35
flooding 15, 16, 18, 20
forests 13-16, 19, 20, 25
fossil fuels 19, 30, 33-35

geology 8, 35
Germany 19
global warming 20, 27, 34
Greenhouse Effect 19, 35

habitats 8, 9, 29
hillwalker syndrome 11, 33
housing 18
human impact 3, 7, 10-23, 26
hunter-gatherers 12

Ice Age 6, 7
ice sheets 6, 7
Indus 26, 32
intensive farming 23, 29, 30, 35
irrigation 17, 22, 25-27, 32

knock-on effects 10, 35

latitude 8, 9
Little Ice Age 7
livestock damage 16, 17

Madagascar 15
making of landscape 4-9
Mayan Empire 26, 27
mining 18
Montreal Protocol 21

Nepal 13, 14

organic farming 30, 35
overgrazing 16, 17, 22
ozone layer 21, 35

Pangaea 6
pesticides 29, 30, 35
plate movement 9

Plato 24, 25
pollution 19, 21, 23
population 11, 13-16, 18, 21, 22, 27, 32, 33
poverty 15
productive land 13

rainforests 5, 14-16, 22, 28
rate of change 6, 10, 20, 21
renewable resources 33-35
resource use 32, 33, 34
rivers 8
rock types 3, 4, 8
Roman Empire 25

Sahara Desert 16
salting 17, 26, 27
sheep 16, 17
shifting agriculture 15, 28, 35
soil 4-6, 8, 13-17, 23-25, 27, 28, 30
soil erosion 13-15, 23, 27, 29
structures 18
Sumerians 25-27

technology 11, 12, 27-29
temperature 19, 20
Third World farming 31, 32
Tibet 5
topography 4, 35
topsoil 13, 14, 23, 29
transportation 11, 12

ultraviolet radiation 21
United States 14, 27

volcanoes 6, 7, 9

waterlogging 17, 22

Photographic Credits:
Cover: Robert Harding Picture Library; pages 2-3, 15, 17 and 31: The Hutchison Library; pages 4-5, 10-11, 14, 20 left, 24-25, 26 and 30: Spectrum Colour Library; pages 6-7, 16, 20 right, 28-29 and 32: The J. Allan Cash Photo Library; page 7: Mary Evans Picture Library; pages 12, 13, 18-19, 21, 26-27, 32-33, 33 and 34: Zefa; page 19: Catherine Bradley.